# What's the Constitution?

Nancy Harris

Heinemann Library
Chicago, IL

**HEINEMANN-RAINTREE**

TO ORDER:

☎ Phone Customer Service **888-454-2279**

💻 Visit **www.heinemannraintree.com** to browse our catalog and order online.

Editorial: Rebecca Rissman
Design: Kimberly R. Miracle and Betsy Wernert
Illustrations: Mapping Specialists
Photo Research: Tracy Cummins and Heather Mauldin
Production: Duncan Gilbert

Originated by Modern Age
Printed in China by South China Printing Company
The paper used to print this book comes from sustainable resources.

ISBN-13: 978-1-4329-0983-3 (hc)
ISBN-10: 1-4329-0983-5 (hc)
ISBN-13: 978-1-4329-0989-5 (pb)
ISBN-10: 1-4329-0989-4 (pb)

12 11 10 09 08
10 9 8 7 6 5 4 3 2 1

**Library of Congress Cataloging-in-Publication Data**
Harris, Nancy.
  What's the U.S. Constitution? / Nancy Harris.
    p. cm. -- (First guide to government)
  Includes bibliographical references and index.
  ISBN 978-1-4329-0983-3 (hc) -- ISBN 978-1-4329-0989-5 (pb)  1.  Constitutional law--United States--Juvenile literature. 2.  Constitutional history--United States--Juvenile literature.  I. Title. II. Title: What's the United States Constitution.
  KF4550.Z9H35 2008
  342.7302'9--dc22
                            2008001155

**Acknowledgments**
The author and publisher are grateful to the following for permission to reproduce copyright material: ©Alamy **p. 5** (Glow Images); ©AP Photo **p. 29** (Ron Edmonds); ©Collection of the Supreme Court of the United States **p. 19**; ©Corbis **pp. 6** (Ken Cedeno), **16** (Gregg Newton), **17** (Tetra Images), **22** (Joe Marquette); ©Getty Images **pp. 7** (Joe Raedle), **11** (MPI); ©Library of Congress Prints and Photographs Division **p. 13**; ©North Wind Picture Archive **p. 9** (North Wind); ©Shutterstock **pp. 21** (Ricardo Garza), **24** (Bob Ainsworth); ©The Granger Collection, New York **pp. 10, 12, 14, 27**; ©The National Archives and Records Administration **p. 4, 23, 25, 28**.

Cover image used with permission of ©Jupiter Images (Tetra Images).

The publishers would like to thank Nancy Harris for her assistance in the preparation of this book.

# Contents

Some words are shown in bold, **like this**. You can find out what they mean by looking in the glossary.

# What Is the United States Constitution?

The United States Constitution is a very important **document** (paper). It was written by a group of men who lived in the United States of America. At the time when the Constitution was written, the United States was a new country.

★★★ The Constitution is four pages long.

★ The capitol of the United States is in Washingon, D.C.

The Constitution was written to explain how the United States **federal government** should work. The federal government leads the entire country. The Constitution is a written **law** (rule) that the federal government must follow.

★ The Constitution gives people the freedom of speech.

The Constitution describes the **rights** of people in the United States. Rights are freedoms that people have. These rights include the right to say what you believe. The **law** of the Constitution must be followed by everyone in the United States.

★ The Constitution gives new citizens rights.

The Constitution can be changed. These changes are called **amendments**. Amendments are made to meet the needs of the country or individual states. They are made to meet the needs of **citizens** in the United States. Citizens are people who live in the United States and can vote for their leaders.

# History of the Constitution

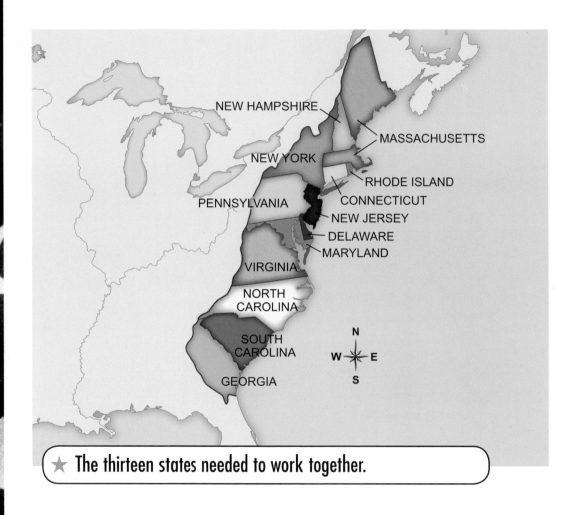

NEW HAMPSHIRE

MASSACHUSETTS

NEW YORK

RHODE ISLAND

CONNECTICUT

PENNSYLVANIA

NEW JERSEY

DELAWARE

MARYLAND

VIRGINIA

NORTH CAROLINA

SOUTH CAROLINA

GEORGIA

★ The thirteen states needed to work together.

When the United States of America first became a country, there were only thirteen states. Each state had its own **document** that said how its **state government** would run the state.

In 1776, people in the states joined together to create the United States. They decided they needed a government to lead all the states. They decided to write a document to create rules for how this government would work.

★ Important people met to create the new government.

# The Articles of Confederation

The document was called the **Articles of Confederation**. It was written in 1781. The Articles of Confederation did not give the government a lot of power over the states. People realized this was not working.

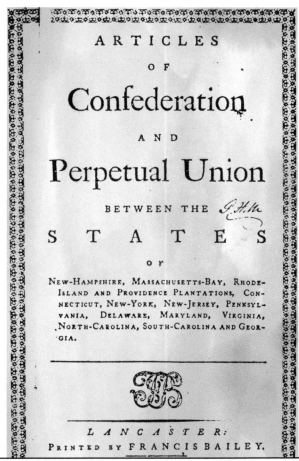

★ This is a printed copy of the Articles of Confederation.

The states needed a stronger government to lead them. They decided to rewrite the Articles of Confederation. They held a meeting in the city of Philadelphia. The meeting was called the **Constitutional Convention**.

★ Leaders met at Independence Hall in Philadelphia.

# Writing the Constitution

The meeting included a man from each state except the state of Rhode Island. People at the meeting decided that they would write a new **document** called the United States Constitution. This document would replace the **Articles of Confederation**.

★★★ State leaders discussed the kind of government they would create.

★ George Washington

★ Benjamin Franklin

★ James Madison

★ Alexander Hamilton

The Constitution was written by a group of men. They decided how the **federal government** would work. Some of these men were James Madison, Alexander Hamilton, George Washington, and Benjamin Franklin.

★ After the Constitution was approved, it was signed.

The United States Constitution was written in 1787. On September 17, 1787, it was **approved** by the men who attended the **Constitutional Convention**. It also had to be accepted by the states.

In order to become a **law**, nine states had to vote in favor of the Constitution. The state of New Hampshire was the ninth state to approve the Constitution. This happened in June of 1788. The Constitution then replaced the **Articles of Confederation**.

Today there are 50 states. They all must obey the law of the US Constitution.

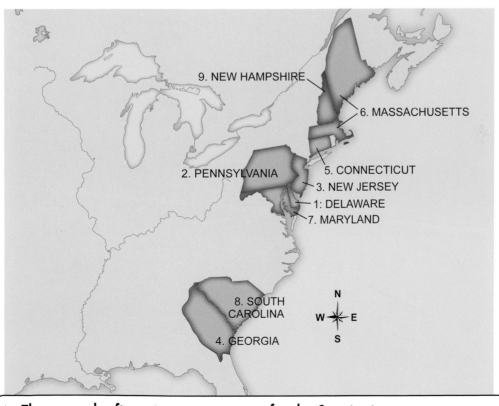

★ These are the first nine states to vote for the Constitution.

# Parts of the Constitution

The United States Constitution has three parts:

- the **preamble** (tells why the Constitution was written)
- the **articles** (tells how the federal government works)
- the **amendments** (lists changes to the Constitution)

⭐ The Constitution is on display in Washington, D.C.

# The Preamble

The preamble is the first part of the Constitution. It explains why the Constitution was written. It was written to form a strong **federal** government.

★ The preamble introduces the Constitution.

# Articles One, Two, and Three: The Federal Government

There are seven **articles** in the Constitution. The first three articles describe how the **federal government** works. The founding fathers divided the federal government into three branches (parts). These are:

- The **legislative branch** (Article One)
- The **executive branch** (Article Two)
- The **judicial branch** (Article Three)

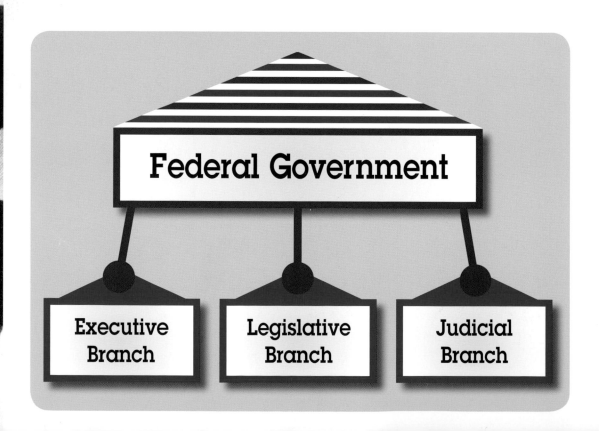

★ These are the Supreme Court Judges.

The first three articles describe the job of each branch of the government. The legislative branch makes laws for the country. The executive branch makes sure the laws are followed. The judicial branch decides if a law has been broken.

★★★ Each part of the federal government meets in Washington, D.C.

The first three **articles** explain how the three branches must work together. The branches have different jobs, but they must agree with the decisions of the other two branches. One branch cannot make decisions for the entire country.

# Article Four: State Governments

Article Four describes how the **state governments** work with the **federal government**. It also describes how states work with each other. Article Four says that each state can make its own **laws**. States must also follow federal laws.

★ Each state has its own government.

# Article Five:
# Changing the Constitution

★★★ The 27th Amendment was the last
amendment added to the Constitution.

The Constitution can be **amended** (changed). Article
Five describes how to amend the Constitution. It takes a
long time to add a new **amendment** to the Constitution.
People in the **federal government** and the states must
vote in favor of the amendment for it to be added.

Article Five helps the government meet the needs of its people.

Article Five makes the Constitution a special document. It allows the Constitution to change when the needs of American **citizens** change. The Constitution can be amended at any time.

# Article Six: Paying Debts

Article Six says that the **federal government** will pay money it owes to other people or countries. This article was written because the founding fathers wanted to be sure to pay any debts owed by the new country.

The Constitution tells Americans that the United States will repay its debts.

## Article Seven: Approving the Constitution

Article Seven explains how the United States Constitution was **ratified** (approved). Nine out of thirteen states had to vote in favor of the Constitution for it to become a **law**. Article Seven includes the signatures of the members of the **Constitutional Convention**. All the members of the convention approved the document.

# The Amendments

The last part of the United States Constitution is the **amendments**. These are changes that have been made to the Constitution. These changes are new **laws** that are added to the Constitution.

The first ten amendments were ratified (approved) on December 15, 1791. They are called the **Bill of Rights**. These ten laws protect people's rights or freedoms. They were added just four years after the Constitution had been written.

# Congress of the United States

*begun and held at the City of New-York, on*

*Wednesday the fourth of March, one thousand seven hundred and eighty nine*

THE Conventions of a number of the States, having at the time of their adopting the Constitution, expressed a desire, in order to prevent misconstruction or abuse of its powers, that further declaratory and restrictive clauses should be added: And as extending the ground of public confidence in the Government, will best ensure the beneficent ends of its institution

RESOLVED by the Senate and House of Representatives of the United States of America, in Congress assembled, two thirds of both Houses concurring, that the following Articles be proposed to the Legislatures of the several States, as amendments to the Constitution of the United States, all, or any of which Articles, when ratified by three fourths of the said Legislatures, to be valid to all intents and purposes, as part of the said Constitution; viz.

ARTICLES in addition to, and Amendment of the Constitution of the United States of America, proposed by Congress, and ratified by the Legislatures of the several States, pursuant to the fifth Article of the original Constitution.

**Article the first....** After the first enumeration required by the first Article of the Constitution, there shall be one Representative for every thirty thousand, until the number shall amount to one hundred, after which, the proportion shall be so regulated by Congress, that there shall be not less than one hundred Representatives, nor less than one Representative for every forty thousand persons, until the number of Representatives shall amount to two hundred, after which the proportion shall be so regulated by Congress, that there shall not be less than two hundred Representatives, nor more than one Representative for every fifty thousand persons.

**Article the second....** No law, varying the compensation for the services of the Senators and Representatives, shall take effect, until an election of Representatives shall have intervened.

**Article the third....** Congress shall make no law respecting an establishment of religion, or prohibiting the free exercise thereof; or abridging the freedom of speech, or of the press; or the right of the people peaceably to assemble, and to petition the Government for a redress of grievances.

**Article the fourth.** A well regulated militia, being necessary to the security of a free State, the right of the people to keep and bear arms, shall not be infringed.

**Article the fifth.** No Soldier shall, in time of peace be quartered in any house, without the consent of the owner, nor in time of war, but in a manner to be prescribed by law.

**Article the sixth.** The right of the people to be secure in their persons, houses, papers, and effects, against unreasonable searches and seizures, shall not be violated, and no Warrants shall issue, but upon probable cause, supported by oath or affirmation, and particularly describing the place to be searched, and the persons or things to be seized.

**Article the seventh.** No person shall be held to answer for a capital, or otherwise infamous crime, unless on a presentment or indictment of a Grand Jury, except in cases arising in the land or naval forces, or in the Militia, when in actual service in time of War or public danger; nor shall any person be subject for the same offence to be twice put in jeopardy of life or limb, nor shall be compelled in any criminal case to be a witness against himself, nor be deprived of life, liberty, or property, without due process of law; nor shall private property be taken for public use, without just compensation.

**Article the eighth.** In all criminal prosecutions, the accused shall enjoy the right to a speedy and public trial, by an impartial jury of the State and district wherein the crime shall have been committed, which district shall have been previously ascertained by law, and to be informed of the nature and cause of the accusation; to be confronted with the witnesses against him; to have compulsory process for obtaining witnesses in his favor, and to have the assistance of Counsel for his defence.

**Article the ninth.** In suits at common law, where the value in controversy shall exceed twenty dollars, the right of trial by jury shall be preserved, and no fact tried by a jury, shall be otherwise re-examined in any Court of the United States, than according to the rules of the common law.

**Article the tenth....** Excessive bail shall not be required, nor excessive fines imposed, nor cruel and unusual punishments inflicted.

**Article the eleventh.** The enumeration in the Constitution, of certain rights, shall not be construed to deny or disparage others retained by the people.

**Article the twelfth.** The powers not delegated to the United States by the Constitution, nor prohibited by it to the States, are reserved to the States respectively, or to the people.

ATTEST,

*Frederick Augustus Muhlenberg, Speaker of the House of Representatives.*

*John Adams, Vice-President of the United States, and President of the Senate.*

*John Beckley, Clerk of the House of Representatives.*

*Sam. A. Otis Secretary of the Senate.*

> ★★★ Ten of the first twelve amendments were approved and became the Bill of Rights.

# Why Is the Constitution Important?

The United States Constitution is the highest **law** in the United States. The Constitution created the **federal government**.

★★★ The Constitution gave people in the United States rights and freedoms.

The Constitution states the rights of people living in the United States. It is written to protect the rights of people living in the United States.

★ You can see the Constitution in Washington, D.C.

# Glossary

**amend**  change a piece of text. You can amend the Constitution by adding a new law.

**amendment**  change made to a piece of writing. The change could be a text change or something that has been added to the text. An amendment to the Constitution is when you add a new law.

**approve**  agree with something

**article**  part or piece of writing in a text. There are seven articles in the US Constitution.

**Articles of Confederation**  document that stated how the government would lead all the states.

**Bill of Rights**  first ten amendments. These changes were added to protect the rights (freedoms) of people who live in the United States.

**citizen**  person who is born in the United States. People who have moved to the United States from another country can become citizens by taking a test.

**Constitutional Convention**  meeting held in the city of Philadelphia. The men at this meeting decided to write the US constitution.

**document**  written text or paper. The US Constitution is a document.

**executive branch**  part of the United States federal government. This branch makes sure the laws in the United States are followed.

**federal government**  group of leaders who run the entire country. In a federal government, the country is made up of many states.

**judicial branch**  part of the United States federal government. This branch makes sure the laws in the country are understood.

**law**  rule people must obey in a state or country

**legislative branch**  part of the United States federal government that makes laws. Congress is the legislative branch.

**preamble**  first part of a text. It is written to tell why the paper was written.

**ratify**  agree with something

**rights**  freedoms that people have. Rights include the right to say and write what you think.

**state government**  group of leaders who run a state. Each state in the United States has a state government.

# Find Out More

## Books to Read

**An older reader can help you with these books:**

Levy, Elizabeth. *If You Were There When They Signed the Constitution.* New York: Scholastic, 2006.

Pearl, Norman. *The Bill of Rights.* Mankato, MN: Picture Window Books, 2007.

Teitelbaum, Michael. *The U.S. Constitution.* Mankato, MN: Child's World, 2005.

## Websites

*Ben's Guide to U.S. Government*
Visit **http://bensguide.gpo.gov/** to play games and learn the ABCs of the United States Government.

## Viewing the US Constitution

The US Constitution is on display in the National Archives in the Rotunda. The rotunda is open daily from 9 am to 5 pm.

*The National Archives address is:*
700 Pennsylvania Avenue, NW
Washington, DC 20408

# Index